Vegan Nice Cre‑   ‑s

56 Guilt Free an‑   ‑na

Ice C‑

Table of Contents

Introduction

Are you looking for a healthy and easy way to enjoy ice cream?

This book is jam packed with 56 guilt free banana ice cream recipes. Nice cream is a simple and healthy treat, perfect for the hot days of summer or just for a sweet treat.

Nice cream is a wonderful replacement for ice cream, but so much healthier. Banana ice cream is low calorie, low fat and all of these recipes are vegan. They all taste healthy and clean, perfect for any weight loss or health journey.

In just minutes you can have a gluten free, paleo friendly and dairy free treat. All you need is a food processor or blender, a few minutes and just a few ingredients. In this book you will find favorite flavors such as mint chocolate, cookie dough, chocolate, peppermint and so much more.

I was recently diagnosed with low thyroid, so I researched these recipes for my own vegan and gluten free lifestyle. If they work for you, great! But feel free to substitute any ingredients.

If you have any questions, I would love to hear from you. Enjoy!

A Few Tips

Here are a few tips that may help you in making the perfect banana ice cream.

- Ripe bananas work best. Luckily, many grocery stores will have ripe bananas for super cheap.
- Make sure to peel your bananas before freezing them. It's MUCH tougher to peel the bananas after freezing them.
- Serve immediately for frozen yogurt consistency. Freeze if want it more like an ice cream consistency.
- In many cases, a good food processor or high quality blender works best with these recipes. Unfortunately, I have found that it's difficult to make these recipes in a cheap blender.
- Feel free to experiment with different flavors and toppings. These recipes are guidelines that I have researched, but there are many different combinations and possibilities.

Double Berry Ice Cream

Makes 2 servings

Ingredients
2 frozen bananas, sliced
¼ tsp vanilla extract
¼ tsp almond extract
¼ cup frozen raspberries
¼ cup frozen blueberries

Directions
1. In a food processor or blender, mix bananas until smooth.
2. Add extracts and berries. Pulse until berries mix.
3. Serve now for frozen yogurt consistency. Freeze if prefer it firm.

Coffee Butter Ice Cream

Makes 6 servings

Ingredients
8 small frozen bananas, sliced
1 cup almond milk
¼ cup almond butter
2 tbsp favorite instant coffee

Directions
1. In a food processor or blender, mix bananas until smooth.
2. In a separate bowl, dissolve the instant coffee in the almond milk.
3. Add to the bananas, along with the almond butter. Mix until smooth.
4. Serve now for frozen yogurt consistency. Freeze if prefer it firm.

Biscoff Cookie Chunk Ice Cream
Makes 1 pint

Ingredients
2 ripe bananas, sliced and frozen
½ cup coconut cream
½ cup Biscoff Spread
6 Biscoff cookies, broken into small chunks

Directions
1. In a food processor or blender, mix bananas, coconut cream and cookie spread until smooth.
2. Pour into a container and mix in the cookie chunks.
3. Freeze for at least 4 hours before serving.

Yummy Salted Caramel Ice Cream
Makes 2 servings

Ingredients
4 frozen bananas, sliced
¼ cup soft dates
Pinch salt
4-5 drops English Toffee stevia drops
(optional)

Directions
1. In a food processor or blender, add all ingredients and blend.
2. Stop and scrape down the sides once or twice to make sure everything blends smoothly.
3. May take several minutes, but final product will be thick and creamy.
4. Serve immediately if prefer frozen yogurt consistency. Freeze if prefer it firm.

Peanut Butter Chocolate Chip Ice Cream

Makes 1 large serving

Ingredients
2 frozen bananas, sliced
2 tbsp natural peanut butter
3 tbsp raw cacao nibs
Pinch sea salt
Splash of almond or coconut milk.

Directions
1. In a food processor or blender, add bananas and mix until it has a crumb-like consistency.
2. Add peanut butter, cacao nibs, sea salt and almond or coconut milk.
3. Mix until creamy.
4. Serve immediately if prefer frozen yogurt consistency. Freeze if prefer it firm.

Mocha Nut Ice Cream
Makes 1 serving

Ingredients
1 frozen banana, sliced or chunked
½ tbsp cocoa powder
¼ tsp espresso powder
1 tbsp chopped nuts (pick your favorite)

Directions
1. In a food processor or blender, add bananas and mix until smooth and creamy.
2. Add coffee and cocoa powder and blend until completely mixed.
3. Stir in chopped nuts.
4. Serve immediately if prefer frozen yogurt consistency. Freeze if prefer it firm.

Banana Berry Ice Cream

Makes 4 servings

Ingredients
2 ripe bananas, sliced and frozen
2 cups mixed frozen berries
¼ cup coconut milk
Lemon juice

Directions
1. In a food processor or blender, add bananas, berries and coconut milk. Mix until smooth and creamy.
2. Stop and scrape down the sides, then continue to blend. Repeat until a smooth ice cream forms.
3. Add a squeeze of lemon.
4. Scoop and serve immediately.

Piña Colada Nice Cream
Makes 1 serving

Ingredients
1 frozen banana, sliced or in chunks
½ cup frozen pineapple chunks
¼ cup coconut milk
2 ice cubes (optional)

Directions
1. In a food processor or blender, add all ingredients and blend until smooth and creamy.
2. If not thick enough, add ice cubes and blend.
3. Serve immediately.

Peanut Butter Crunch Ice Cream

Makes 2 servings

Ingredients
2 frozen bananas, sliced
2 tbsp natural peanut butter
2 tbsp pure maple syrup
¼ tsp pure vanilla extract
1-2 tbsp almond milk
¼ cup pretzels, chopped

Directions
1. In a food processor or blender, add bananas, peanut butter, maple syrup and vanilla. Blend until smooth and creamy.
2. If mix is too thick or unable to blend smoothly, add almond milk and continue mixing.
3. Add crushed pretzels and freeze for 10 minutes.
4. Serve and enjoy!

Coconut Chai Ice Cream
Makes 2-3 servings

Ingredients
3 frozen ripe bananas, sliced or chunked
5 tbsp coconut cream or coconut milk
1¼ tsp cinnamon
2 tsp fresh ginger, minced
1 tsp vanilla extract

Directions
1. In a food processor or blender, add all ingredients and mix until smooth.
2. You may need to stop and press mixture down the sides.
3. Enjoy immediately for frozen yogurt consistency. For an ice cream consistency, freeze for an hour.

Banana Custard Ice Cream
Makes 3-4 servings

Ingredients
4 frozen bananas, sliced or chunked
¼ cup vegan milk
1 tsp vanilla extract
6 vanilla cookies

Directions
1. In a food processor or blender, add bananas and mix for 2 minutes.
2. Add vegan milk and vanilla. Mix again.
3. Use a spatula and push ice cream around and away from the sides.
4. Add more milk and mix until smooth. Use spatula if needed.
5. Break half of the cookies into chunks and mix into the ice cream.
6. Break the rest of the cookies into chunks and stir into the ice cream.
7. Serve immediately or freeze until ready to enjoy.

Mint Chocolate Nice Cream
Makes 2-3 servings

Ingredients
3 frozen bananas
¼ tsp spirulina powder
¼ tsp vanilla powder
¼ cup mint leaves
¼ cup almond milk
¼ cup dark chocolate chunks, melted

Directions
1. In a food processor or blender, blend all ingredients except for the chocolate chunks.
2. Continue blending until smooth and creamy.
3. Scoop and drizzle with melted chocolate.

Date the Tahini Ice Cream
Makes 3 servings

Ingredients
½ cup raw tahini
4- 6 medjool dates, pitted
3 frozen bananas, sliced
¼ cup vegan milk (choose your favorite)

Directions
1. In a blender or food processor, blend all ingredients until smooth.
2. If prefer a soft serve consistency, scoop and serve immediately.
3. If prefer it more like ice cream, freeze until set.

Mouthwatering Watermelon Ice Cream

Makes 1-2 servings

Ingredients
2-3 frozen bananas
1-2 cups frozen watermelon chunks
½ - 1 cup non-dairy milk (use as little as possible)

Directions
1. In a blender or food processor, blend all ingredients until smooth and creamy.
2. For best results, serve immediately and enjoy!

Tropical Whip Ice Cream
Makes 1-2 servings

Ingredients
2 cups frozen pineapple
1 frozen banana, sliced
2 tbsp unsweetened almond milk

Directions
1. In a blender or food processor, blend all ingredients. Every minute or so, stop and scrape down the sides with a spatula.
2. After several minutes, mixture should be smooth and creamy.
3. Serve immediately for best results. Enjoy as-is, or add your own toppings for a personal creation.

Delightful Coconut Banana Ice Cream
Makes 4 servings

Ingredients
2 frozen bananas, sliced
Whipped coconut cream
Shaved dark chocolate for garnish, optional

Directions
1. In a blender or food processor, blend the bananas until it's a crumby texture.
2. Add half the cream and blend until mixed together.
3. Add the rest of the cream and blend until it's a creamy, frozen yogurt consistency.
4. Scoop into four small bowls and garnish with dark chocolate if desired.

Simply Rich Peanut Butter Chocolate Ice Cream

Makes 1-2

Ingredients
2 frozen bananas, sliced
2 tbsp peanut butter
1 tbsp cocoa powder
Almond milk or water (optional)

Directions
1. Place bananas into a blender or food processor. Blend until smooth.
2. If needed, add a little almond milk or water to make the process a little easier.
3. You may need to open the processor or blender and stir.
4. Once creamy, add the peanut butter and cocoa powder.
5. Mix well.
6. Serve immediately and enjoy!

Apple Cinnamon Delight Ice Cream
Makes 1 large serving

Ingredients
2 frozen bananas, sliced
¼ cup apple butter
¼ tsp vanilla extract
¼ tsp ground cinnamon

Directions
1. In a food processor or blender, add banana slices and pulse until smooth.
2. You may need to scrape the sides occasionally with a spatula.
3. Add the rest of the ingredients and pulse until combined.
4. Serve and enjoy!

Basic Chocolate Soft Serve

Makes 1 large serving

Ingredients
2 frozen bananas, sliced
1 tbsp unsweetened cocoa powder
¼ teaspoon vanilla extract

Directions
1. In a food processor or blender, add ingredients and mix until smooth.
2. If needed, stop and scrape the sides occasionally with a spatula.
3. Continue mixing until smooth and creamy.
4. Serve and enjoy!

Pumpkin Spice Ice Cream
Makes 1 large serving

Ingredients
2 frozen bananas, sliced
2 tbsp apple butter
⅓ cup pure pumpkin puree (Organic if possible)
¼ tsp pumpkin pie spice

Directions
1. In a food processor or blender, add banana slices and pulse until smooth.
2. You may need to scrape the sides occasionally with a spatula.
3. Add the rest of the ingredients and pulse until combined.
4. Serve immediately or freeze for 15 for a firm texture.

Almond Butter Banana Soft Serve

Makes 4 servings

Ingredients
5 frozen bananas, sliced
½ cup almond butter

Directions
1. In a food processor or blender, add banana slices and mix until smooth.
2. Add almond butter and blend until completely mixed.
3. Serve immediately or freeze for 1-2 hours for a firmer consistency.

Old Fashioned Strawberry Banana Soft Serve

Makes 1 large serving

Ingredients
1 frozen banana, sliced
½ cup frozen strawberries
½ tsp vanilla extract

Directions
1. In a food processor or blender, add all ingredients and mix until smooth.
2. You may need to scrape the sides occasionally with a spatula.
3. Serve immediately and enjoy!

Peanut Butter and Bananas Soft Serve

Makes 1-2 servings

Ingredients
2 frozen bananas, sliced
2 tbsp natural peanut butter
Pinch of sea salt

Directions
1. In a food processor or blender, add all ingredients and mix until smooth.
2. You may need to scrape the sides occasionally with a spatula.
3. Serve immediately and enjoy!

Carrot Cake Soft Serve

Makes 1-2 servings

INGREDIENTS

1 frozen banana, sliced

¼ cup apple butter

1 large carrot, peeled and grated

¼ tsp vanilla extract

2 tbsp raisins

2 tbsp chopped walnuts

Directions

1. In a food processor or blender, add bananas and mix until smooth.
2. You may need to scrape the sides occasionally with a spatula.
3. Add the apple butter, carrot and vanilla. Mix until just combined.
4. Add the raisins and walnuts.
5. Serve immediately or freeze for 15-20 minutes for a firm consistency.

Cherry Coconut Ice Cream
Makes 4-5 servings

Ingredients
4 frozen bananas, chopped
2 cups frozen cherries
1¼ cup coconut milk (If you have a powerful blender or food processor, you may not need so much)
Coconut flakes (optional)

Directions
1. In a food processor or blender, add bananas and cherries. Add coconut milk slowly and continue to mix until smooth and creamy.
2. You may need to scrape the sides occasionally with a spatula.
3. Serve and add coconut flakes if desired.

Healthy Chocolate Chip Delight Soft Serve

Makes 2-3 servings

INGREDIENTS
3 frozen bananas, sliced
¼ cup unsweetened almond or coconut milk
1 tbsp maple syrup
2 tbsp raw cacao powder
2 tbsp vegan chocolate chips
your favorite toppings: I used banana slices, extra chocolate chips, granola and chia seeds

Directions
1. In a food processor or blender, add bananas and coconut or almond milk. Pulse and scrape down the sides when needed.
2. Continue until it's smooth and creamy. It may take several minutes.
3. Add the rest of the ingredients and mix until combined well.

Heavenly Peanut Butter Fudge Swirl

Makes 4-5 servings

Ingredients

Fudge Chunks:

¾ cup coconut flour

¼ cup cocoa powder

½ cup maple syrup

1 tsp pure vanilla extract

¼ tsp sea salt

Ice Cream Base:

6 frozen bananas, sliced

1 cup natural peanut butter

6 tbsp maple syrup

1 tsp pure vanilla extract

1 tsp sea salt

Directions

1. In a food processor, add all of the fudge ingredients and mix until it resembles dry brownie batter.
2. Put on a plate and break some of the mixture into finer pieces.

3. Combine all ice cream ingredients in the food processor until creamy.
4. Add the rest of the ingredients and pulse just long enough so the fudge chunks are mixed throughout.
5. Serve and enjoy.

Cantaloupe Soft Serve
Makes 1 large serving

Ingredients
¼ cantaloupe melon
1 frozen banana, sliced

Directions
1. In a food processor or blender, add all of the ingredients.
2. Blend until completely smooth.
3. Serve and enjoy!

Peanut Butter Cookie Chunk Ice Cream

Makes 2 servings

Ingredients
4 frozen bananas, sliced
8 oreo cookies
2 tbsp chunky peanut butter
2 tbsp peanuts

Directions
1. In a food processor or blender, add the bananas, peanut butter and 3 of the cookies and blend until smooth.
2. Add 3 more cookies and mix for about 5 seconds.
3. Serve in 2 bowls and top it with the rest of the cookies and peanuts.

Cookie Dough Soft Serve
Makes 8 servings

Ingredients
⅓ cup garbanzo beans
2 tbsp natural peanut butter
1½ tbsp powdered peanut butter
1 tsp agave nectar
½ tsp raw vanilla extract
¼ tsp cinnamon
Pinch of sea salt
1 tbsp dairy-free chocolate chips
6 large frozen bananas, sliced

Directions
1. In a small food processor, add the garbanzo beans, peanut butter, peanut butter powder, agave, vanilla, cinnamon and sea salt.
2. Mix until creamy. You may need to scrape the sides often for easier mixing.
3. Transfer to a bowl and stir in the chocolate chips.

4. Line a plate with parchment paper. Roll the cookie dough into extremely small pieces and put on the plate.
5. Place into freezer and remove when hardened, about 30 minutes.
6. In a food processor or blender, add the bananas and blend until smooth.
7. Add bananas into a large bowl and stir in cookie dough.
8. Serve and enjoy.

Sour Grapefruit Soft Serve
Makes 2 servings

Ingredients
2 frozen bananas, sliced
½ cup frozen grapefruit, peeled and sliced
¼ cup frozen purple seedless grapes

Directions
1. In a food processor or blender, add half the bananas, half the grapefruit and the grapes. Blend until smooth.
2. Add the rest of the ingredients and blend until creamy
3. Serve and enjoy!

Chocolate Lovers Soft Serve
Makes 4-6 servings

Ingredients
2 frozen bananas, sliced
½ cup cocoa powder
1 cup almond or cashew milk
½ cup non-dairy chocolate chips plus a little more for topping
chocolate sprinkles, for topping

Directions
1. In a food processor or blender, add all of the ingredients, except for the toppings. Blend until smooth.
2. Scoop into bowls, top with the remaining chocolate chips and sprinkles.
3. Serve and enjoy!

Mocha Chip Nice Cream
Makes 4 servings

Ingredients
4-5 frozen bananas, chopped
1 tsp instant espresso or coffee powder
2 tbsp unsweetened cocoa powder
¼ cup vegan chocolate chips

Directions
1. In a food processor or blender, add bananas and blend until smooth.
2. Add coffee, cocoa powder and mix completely.
3. Stir in chocolate chips.
4. Serve immediately or freeze for a firm consistency.

Coffee Ice Cream

Makes 1-2 servings

Ingredients
¼ cup of very strong espresso coffee
Sugar or stevia (optional)
3 frozen bananas, sliced
½ tsp vanilla extract

Directions
1. Make the coffee and sweeten to your preferred taste
2. In a food processor or blender, add bananas, coffee and vanilla extract.
3. Blend until creamy.
4. Freeze for an hour.
5. Serve and enjoy.

Spiced Banana Nut Ice Cream
Makes 2 servings

Ingredients
1 cup walnuts
1 tbsp coconut oil
1-2 frozen banana, sliced
2 medjool dates, pitted
½ tsp ground cinnamon
Pinch of freshly ground nutmeg
1 tbsp chia seeds
1 tbsp cacao nibs
Toppings: extra walnuts (crushed) and extra cacao nibs

Directions
1. Add walnuts to a blender and pulse for a few seconds.
2. Add the coconut oil, dates, cinnamon, nutmeg and frozen banana to the walnuts. Blend until creamy and smooth.
3. Scoop the soft serve into a bowl and use a spoon to mix in the chia seeds and cacao nibs.

4. Sprinkle the extra walnuts and cacao nibs on top and place in the freezer overnight.
5. If you can't wait a day to eat the ice cream, serve immediately. However, it will be a little softer.
6. Either way you choose, enjoy!

Dark Chocolate Coconut Banana Ice Cream

Makes 2 servings

Ingredients
3 medium frozen bananas, sliced or chunked
2 tbsp dark chocolate chips
1 tsp coconut flakes
1 tsp sliced almonds
1 tsp dark chocolate shavings (optional)

Directions
1. Add bananas and dark chocolate chips to a blender or food processor. Blend until smooth and creamy.
2. Scoop the ice cream into 2 bowls.
3. Top with the coconut, almonds and chocolate shavings.
4. Serve and enjoy!

Gingerbread Soft Serve

Makes 3-4 servings

Ingredients
8 frozen bananas, sliced
¼ cup agave
1 tsp ground ginger
1 tsp ground cinnamon
1 tsp vanilla extract
1 tsp lemon juice
6-8 vegan gingerbread cookies, crumbled

Directions
1. In a blender or food processor, blend everything except the cookies. Continue until creamy and smooth.
2. Add about ⅓ of the cookie crumbles. Blend just long enough to combine.
3. Pour mixture into a shallow dish and sprinkle about half the remaining cookie crumbles on top.
4. Freeze for 2-3 hours.
5. Scoop into bowls and top with the remaining cookie crumbles.
6. Serve and enjoy!

Peanut Butter Banana Nut Ice Cream

Makes 2 servings

Ingredients
3 large frozen bananas, sliced
3 tbsp natural peanut butter
¼ tsp vanilla extract
Dash of cinnamon
Sea salt, to taste
Roasted peanuts, for topping

Directions
1. In a blender or food processor, add the bananas and blend until smooth and creamy.
2. Add the peanut butter, vanilla extract, cinnamon and sea salt. Pulse quickly to mix the ingredients together.
3. Scoop and top with peanuts.
4. Serve and enjoy!

Vanilla Avocado Soft Serve with Pistachios

Makes 2 servings

Ingredients
2 frozen bananas, sliced
½ ripe avocado
¼ cup pistachios
1 tbsp shredded coconut
½ tsp pure vanilla extract
¼ tsp almond extract

Directions
1. If the pistachios are still in their shells, remove them and measure ¼ cup.
2. Crush them with something flat and set the nuts aside for later.
3. In a blender or food processor, add all of the ingredients except for the pistachios. Blend until smooth and creamy.
4. Spoon into bowls and add the pistachios on top.

Banana Mango Soft Serve
Makes 4 servings

Ingredients
2 frozen bananas, sliced
2 cups frozen mangos
⅓ cup coconut milk

Directions
1. In a blender or food processor, add all of the ingredients except for the coconut milk.
2. Slowly add the coconut milk and continue to blend until smooth and creamy.
3. Serve and enjoy!

Cherry Banana Soft Serve
Makes 2 servings

Ingredients
2 ripe frozen bananas, sliced
1 cup frozen cherries

Toppings
Organic coconut flakes
Raw organic cacao nibs

Directions
1. In a blender or food processor, add the bananas and cherries.
2. Blend until smooth and creamy.
3. Scoop into bowls. Top with coconut flakes and cacao nibs.
4. Serve and enjoy!

Dark Chocolate Chunk Peanut Butter Ice Cream
Makes 3-4 servings

Ingredients
4 frozen bananas, sliced
2 tbsp dark chocolate chips
2 tbsp cocoa powder, dark or regular
2 tbsp natural peanut butter
Pinch sea salt
Pinch cinnamon

Directions
1. In a blender or food processor, add all of the ingredients. Blend until smooth and creamy.
2. Serve immediately if you prefer a soft serve consistency. If you prefer a firmer consistency, freeze for 1-2 hours.

Blackberry Banana Delight
Makes 3 servings

Ingredients
2 frozen sliced bananas, sliced
1 cup frozen blackberries
2 tbsp agave
½ cup almond or coconut milk (optional)

Directions
1. In a blender or food processor, add all of the ingredients, except for the milk. Blend until smooth and creamy.
2. You may need to stop and stir it a couple of times. If needed, add a little bit of the almond or coconut milk slowly. This will make it easier to mix.
3. Serve and enjoy!

Salted Peanut Butter Banana Ice Cream with Chocolate Caramel Sauce

Makes 2 servings

Ingredients
For the ice cream:
3 frozen bananas, sliced
2 tbsp natural peanut butter
1/4 tsp sea salt

For the chocolate caramel sauce:
4 tbsp of brown rice syrup
2 tbsp of unsweetened cocoa powder

Chopped peanuts for garnish

Directions
1. Mix the brown rice syrup and cocoa powder and heat on low.
2. At the same time, add the bananas and peanut butter to a blender or food processor. Pulse until creamy. Make sure to keep an eye on the caramel sauce so it doesn't burn.

3. When ice cream is almost mixed, add the sea salt a little at a time.
4. Scoop the ice cream into bowls, drizzle the caramel sauce and add nuts.
5. Enjoy!

Mint Chocolate Chunk Soft Serve
Makes 3-4 servings

Ingredients
4-5 frozen bananas, sliced
1/4 tsp mint extract
1 handful of spinach
1-2 tbsp of favorite vegan milk
¼ cup of vegan chocolate chips

Directions
1. In a blender or food processor, add the bananas, mint extract, vegan milk and spinach. Mix until creamy and smooth.
2. Stir in the chocolate chips.
3. Serve immediately and enjoy!

Almond Butter Pecan Ice Cream

Makes 3-4 servings

Ingredients
3-4 frozen bananas, sliced
½ cup almond butter
¼ cup tahini
1 tsp cinnamon
2 tsp vanilla extract
1 cup pecans

Directions
1. In a blender or food processor add all the ingredients, except for the pecans. Mix until creamy and smooth. You may need to stop and scrape down the sides a couple of times.
2. Stir in pecans and pour into an airtight container. Place in the freezer for at least 6 hours to harden.
3. Let sit for about 10 minutes before serving.

Strawberry Banana Mango Ice Cream

Makes 2 servings

Ingredients
2 frozen bananas, sliced
1½-2 cups frozen mango chunks
1 cup whole frozen strawberries

Directions
1. In a blender or food processor, mix the fruit to make a smooth and creamy ice cream. You may need to stop and scrape down the sides a couple of times.
2. Once it's combined and smooth, scoop and enjoy!

Tropical Spinach Ice Cream
Makes 2-3 servings

Ingredients
2 frozen bananas, sliced
¾ cup frozen mango chunks
¼ cup frozen pineapple chunks
1 cup spinach, packed
1 tbsp almond milk

Directions
1. In a blender or food processor, add all of the ingredients. Blend until smooth and creamy.
2. Serve and enjoy immediately!

Protein Filled Ice Cream
Makes 2 servings

Ingredients
2 frozen bananas, sliced
½ cup frozen strawberries
2 tbsp unsweetened almond milk
1 scoop vanilla plant-based protein powder
1 tbsp raw almonds, chopped

Directions
1. In a blender or food processor, add the bananas, strawberries and almond milk. Blend until completely smooth.
2. Add the protein powder and mix for another minute.
3. Serve, top with the chopped almonds and enjoy!

Simple Blueberry Banana Ice Cream

Makes 4 servings

Ingredients
4 frozen bananas, sliced
1 cup blueberries

Directions
1. In a blender or food processor, add the bananas and blueberries. Blend until smooth and creamy.
2. Pour into an airtight container and freeze until firm.
3. Remove from freezer and let it thaw at room temperature for 5 to 10 minutes.
4. Scoop and enjoy!

Green Tea Ice Cream
Makes 2 servings

Ingredients
3 frozen bananas, sliced
1 tbsp almond or cashew milk
2 tsp matcha

Directions
1. In a blender or food processor, add the bananas and blend until slightly chunky.
2. Add milk and matcha. Continue to blend until smooth and creamy.
3. For a soft consistency, serve immediately.
4. Pour into a container and freeze for at least an hour if you prefer a more firm consistency.

Pumpkin Pie Ice Cream
Makes 4 servings

Ingredients
4 frozen bananas, sliced
3 tbsp pumpkin puree
2 tsp pumpkin pie spice

Directions
1. In a blender or food processor, add all of the ingredients. Blend until smooth and creamy.
2. Depending on your blender or food processor, you may need to stop and scrape the sides in order to mix the ingredients completely.
3. Pour ice cream into a container and freeze for 1-2 hours.
4. Remove and allow ice cream to thaw for 5-10 minutes.
5. Serve and enjoy!

Sour Cherry Ice Cream
Makes 5-6 servings

Ingredients
2 cups frozen cherries, unsweetened (make sure to remove the pits and stems)
2 frozen bananas, sliced
1 tbsp agave
1 package firm tofu
1 tsp vanilla
1 tsp lemon juice

Directions
1. In a blender or food processor, add all of the ingredients. Blend until smooth and creamy.
2. Scoop and serve immediately.

Cherry Chocolate Chip Ice Cream
Makes 5 servings

Ingredients
4 frozen bananas, sliced
2 cups of pitted frozen cherries
½ cup of vegan chocolate chips

Directions
1. In a blender or food processor, add the bananas and cherries. Blend until smooth and creamy.
2. Pour into a container and mix in the chocolate chips.
3. Serve immediately for a soft consistency, or freeze if you prefer it more firm.

Sweet Potato Ice Cream
Makes 3 servings

Ingredients
3 frozen bananas, sliced
½ cup mashed sweet potato (make sure it's smooth)
1 tbsp almond butter
½ tsp pure vanilla extract
½ tsp ground cinnamon
¼ tsp ground nutmeg
Pinch sea salt

Directions
1. Add all of the ingredients to a blender or food processor.
2. Blend for a few minutes until it's smooth and creamy.
3. Serve and enjoy!

Peppermint Ice Cream
Makes 3-4 servings

Ingredients
4 frozen bananas, sliced
Dash of unsweetened almond milk
¼ cup unsweetened cocoa powder
1 tsp pure vanilla extract
1-3 drops peppermint extract

Directions
1. In a food processor or blender, add the bananas with the almond milk. Mix until blended.
2. Add the cocoa powder and vanilla extract. Blend.
3. Slowly add one drop of peppermint, mix and taste. Add more if desired.
4. Once it's at your desired taste, serve and enjoy!

About the Author

Hi! I'm Kelli Rae - I'm a vegan and I love to work out in the gym. However, we are all so busy and who really wants to spend tons of time in the kitchen or the gym!??! Being a vegan and gym lover does not have to be complicated, take a lot of time or taste disgusting. Personally, I like to make everything as simple and as quick as possible so I can enjoy life. Need some guidance? Just grab one of my books and see how you can make it a WHOLE LOT EASIER!

If you have any comments or questions, I'd love to help! Send me an email at kelliraefit@gmail.com.

Have a super wonderful day!

Printed in Great Britain
by Amazon